# PRIMATES FROM AN ARCHIPELAGO

Irene Suico Soriano

Published by Rabbit Fool Press

Copyright © 2017 by Irene Suico Soriano

All rights reserved. No part of this book may be reproduced or transmitted in any form by any means without permission in writing from the publisher and/or author who owns the work, except by a reviewer, who may use the contents in a review.

Poems in this work have been published previously in the following publications: *Amerasia Journal, APIAHM Calendar & Cultural Guide, Babaylan, Clamour Dyke Zine, Disorient Journalzine, Father Poems, Flip Magazine, Flippin' Filipinos on American, LA Enkanto Kollective – In Our Blood CD, LA Miscellany, LA Culture Net, LA Telephone Book Vol. 1, Maganda, Our Own Voice Literary e-zine, PacTies, Tea and Tattered Pages, Philippines Free Press, Pinaytration, Short Fuse, Solidarity Journal, The World is Yours!, Traffic Report, and Interlope #8.*

Cover artwork by Tala Oliver Mateo, "\_\_\_\_\_ or \_\_\_\_\_", watercolor
Author Photo by Barbra Ramos

Rabbit Fool Press
www.rabbitfoolpress.com
ISBN 978-1-7751789-0-3

# PRAISE FOR PRIMATES FROM AN ARCHIPELAGO

"Soriano's curatorial prowess strikes again... and again, and again. This devastating book of poems will leave you floored, as she delivers heartbreaking stories of family and home, of loss and yet of fulfillment, and memories of bygone days in a city that will soon cease to exist underneath the formidable tumors of a colonial cancer that has ravaged much of the earth — but a city perpetually in the throes of reproduction. Soriano is a deft writer whose words will revive the fight in you. Not only has she accomplished the immortalization of these histories and its people who refuse to be disappeared, she raises from the dead voices that will forever ring through the racket of globalization."
—Jolie Chea, scholar-activist

"These poems are resurrections of dreams lost, meditations on the ways we adapt, surrender, resist, prevail. They are migrations that reveal the 'lies about our comfortable temperatured rooms,' and the redemptive power of love. Irene Suico Soriano writes with great skill and even greater courage."
—Nana-Ama Danquah, author of *Willow Weep for Me*

"The poems in *Primates from an Archipelago* are irresistible. These pages are filled with images so lush and skillful, they carry the imagination dangerously to the brink of falling into pleasure, but watch out for the painful message that the truth kicks us with from these stories."
—Janice Mirikitani, San Francisco's Poet Laureate, 2000

"Irene Suico Soriano marks the distance between the classroom of uniformed children to the women, some of them widows who stare through storefront windows. Fathers and Brothers all in search of a language once spoken in secret. This is the language she paints across the heart of the city: Lincoln Heights periphery detours head on into downtown traffic in central Luzon. Glossy calendar pages are torn from the wall of Memory. Stars once suspended in night sky, she pours inside pale blue envelopes marked 'personal,' poems like anniversary petals pressed between the self, poems transparent as skin."
—Marisela Norte, author of *Peeping Peeping Tom Tom Girl*

*for my family trees*
*Mindanao, Visayas, Luzon*
*Romo-Murphy ... Mendoza-Suico ... Valdez-Soriano*
*... all roots ...*

+++

*for the Silver Spring monkeys*
*Chester, Paul, Billy, Hard Times, Domitian, Nero, Titus,*
*Big Boy, Augustus, Allen, Montaigne, Sisyphus, Charlie,*
*Brooks, Hayden, and Adidas*
*... uprooted ...*

## Contents

**SCATTERED ISLANDS**
- 9    Women in Provinces Howling
- 11   Letters of Dead Children Have Come Home — circa 1972
- 13   Safehouses
- 15   Shanghaied: Conversations with the Marikina Police
- 17   Balitaan
- 19   Edge of the Archipelago

**RECLAMATION**
- 31   Abaca Queen and Battery "Murphy" and a Mariveles Moonlit Night
- 32   Zamboangeña Exoticas
- 33   Papa's Back
- 34   Nene
- 35   Antoinette
- 36   Dear Emanuella

**SCATTERED CITIES**
- 41   A London Adolescence
- 42   Staircases
- 43   A Virgin Sings Her Song
- 44   Sons
- 45   In Finding Père Lachaise
- 46   A New Way of Seeing Things
- 47   Dear Martin
- 48   Breathe (the capitalist whirr)
- 49   A Rat Got Out
- 50   The Small-Town Dictator

**SMOG**
- 55   Months
- 57   One of the Worst Days
- 58   Rock/Adept/Water
- 59   Let Me Tell You
- 61   To a White Woman in the Greyhound Station, Sacramento
- 62   Los Angeles Pilipinas
- 65   Off Rampart
- 67   A Second Sky
- 69   uneasy
- 70   Frederick
- 71   Lorena
- 72   Tata Dinong
- 74   Mar'
- 77   Bing
- 84   Lorena | *Eudocia*  2001 | *2017*
- 85   Why This Lost Place

90   THE SHAPE OF MY POETRY

Crab-eating macaque (Macaca fascicularis)
Davao, Philippines, May 2013
Photo courtesy of S. Shankar

THE SILVER SPRING MONKEYS
In 1981, 16 crab-eating macaque monkeys were imported from the Philippines to the Institute for Behavioral Research (IBR) lab in Silver Spring, Maryland for use in cruel scientific research. The groundbreaking discovery by PETA co-founder Alex Pacheco as a volunteer student lab worker led to the nation's first arrest and criminal conviction of an animal experimenter for cruelty to animals, the first confiscation of abused animals from a laboratory, and the first U.S. Supreme Court victory for animals used in experiments.
https://www.peta.org/issues/animals-used-for-experimentation/silver-spring-monkeys

# Scattered Islands

> *It is not enough just to be outraged.*
> *Injustice has to actually be defied.*
> — Keeanga-Yamahtta Taylor, 2017

# Women in Provinces Howling

You who wanted to be a doctor
butchered, battered, beaten
stripped naked, centered
legs apart.

You who were waiting to be
asked to your first dance
cornered, fondled, sore
thrown across a table mutilated.

You with children learning
their first words,
picked on, kicked, slapped
by men with guns in
green uniform.

*KURA!*
*KURA!*
*KURA!*

You who were promised factory jobs
hauled in boats
shipped out to
new countries
to stations
full of men
*Kizo!*
*Hai!*
no stopping
*Yoneo!*
*Hai!*
no resting
*Yano!*
*Hai!*
*Kitano!*
*Hai!*
performing
*Homma!*
*Hai!*
moaning rhythms
that go on
and on
and on
and on
and on.
Here and now
each
face,
each
green
uniform,
each
black
eye,

each
groan,
nudge,
suck,
and
shiver
must come forth.

No room here for shame or decency,
there are 49 years of evidence to be prepared.

# Letters of Dead Children Have Come Home — circa 1972

Those waiting
for the nun and her parcels
waited by the pews.
While gathering the countless
forms and letters
she brewed tsa.
The charred smell
enveloped the small room
along with her hope that the weight
of terror and sorrow belonging
to those waiting outside
would collapse
under its heavy sweet smell,
sink into the convent grounds
and unburden the small room.

Those from the outside walked in
*The sweet smell doesn't belong here*
*Brew the tsa elsewhere ...*
*Brew the tsa elsewhere ...*

+++

Parcel No.81

<u>Medico-Legal Necrosy Report</u>˙

Name: HILAO, Liliosa R.          Sex: Female
Age: 23                          Occupation: Student
Reported Place of Death:         Constabulary Station Hospital
                                 Camp Crame, Quezon City
Cause of Death:                  Acid Poisoning
Case No.:                        M-432-73

Postmortem findings:
The epiglottis and first portion of the trachea are eroded.
The bronchi are filled with frothy fluid. Cause of death is
cardiorespiratory arrest due to shock with pulmonary edema
as a result of widespread corrosion of the intestinal tract,
Epiglottis and trachea with perforations of the greater
curvature of the stomach.

NOTED: t/GREGORIO MANASAN
             Colonel MC PC (GSC)
             Officer-In-Charge

+++

Approximately one-third of the population of the Greater Manila Area are slum-dwellers. Meanwhile, the president's wife, who was named Governor of Manila in December 1975, had launched a campaign to rid the city of squatters in order to make Manila beautiful, openly admitting that the beautification is especially intended for tourists and foreign investors.˙

+++

Students from the University of the Philippines began to support the demands of the workers and the urban poor, and a massive multi-sector demonstration was planned for the end of January. That month, the military picked up leaders among the students, professionals, workers, and the urban poor. The demonstration had to be postponed.*

+++

No one but no one has been tortured ... None has reason to complain that his dignity has been violated, or that his convenience has not been looked after.
    --President Marcos in a nationwide radio-television address on December 11, 1974.*

---

*Source: Task Force Data Gathering of the Association of Major Religious Superiors in the Philippines, *Political Detainees In The Philippines* (1976)

# Safehouses

*after Manuel Puig*

DAY 5
I mentioned the poet from Macchu Pichu, you said you've read all his works.
You mentioned the priest from Zamboanga, I knew where they were hiding him.
Exchanging life events that made that small room expand
that made you forget about armalites, guerilla tactics, tourniquets, and CB radios,
made me forget about revolutions, newswires, executions, and newspapers.

DAY 9
I said: *Writing is the net that catches my falling life.*
You laughed.
You asked: *Why always tragedy?*

DAY 11
She told me that places have always taken care of her—
from the green, quiet mountains of Badian
to the green, boisterous mountains by Davao.
She dreamt of other places ... there was one ...

DAY 12
You said: *Insurgency is inevitable under increased militarization.*
I laughed.
I asked: *Why always political?*

DAY 14
I told her that places have always taken care of me—
from the bustling streets of Manila
to the comfortable avenues of Paris.
I've dreamt of other places ... like the one she told me ...

DAY 19
It is the one evening we are allowed to go out into the veranda
and I tell you about Gibran's Selma
and other stories of life-lasting love.
You cried quietly under that peaceful night, making me want to embrace
you, and I did.

DAY 65
I am sitting in a hotel room with a window overlooking
a brown river in the middle of this old, sprawling city
you always dreamt of going to
wrapped in a thick, brown woolen jacket you've
always wanted to own and typhoons and humidity
Davao would not allow.
I lie in this hotel room bed, safe, my eyes resting on the inverted portrait
of this city's pride, Bonaparte.
I think of revolutions and what you said, laughing:
*They have abandoned barricades and have returned to perfume.*

DAY 66
I imagine you behind a balete tree, safe
but ears always diligent, listening for approaching vehicles.
You may still be hiding in a delicadeza moonlight
telling someone else
about your beloved Badian
and its coral reefs and
luscious green cogon
this somewhere I will always dream of going.

# Shanghaied: Conversations with the Marikina Police

And so
three days later
neighbors disturbed by
a foul odor,
found
hidden
in the
tall
grass
on a
vacant lot
not far from her
home
Juvelyn's de-
composed
body,
her bandana
tied around her
neck.
She had been punched in the face
so hard her false
teeth
broke
into three pieces.
Pieces later found about
10 meters away
from the grass.

+++

Realizing
Myra
recognized him
even with
the mask, he
found a broken
bottle and
thrust it
into her
sex organ.
In her square
shirt pocket,
the address
of her Aunt's
home.
She was
found
like a
package
identified
and
ready
to be
delivered
home.

+++

Fathers, uncles, brothers, cousins and in-laws were brought in.
Fathers, uncles, brothers, cousins and in-laws were questioned.
Fathers, uncles, brothers, cousins and in-laws were released.

# Balitaan

*(In memory of Flor Contemplacion and Delia Maga, with the thought that they were friends before the Singaporean government accused and convicted Flor of Delia's murder.)*

*MARICRIS SIOSON: died on September 19, 1991, allegedly of hepatitis. Her body bore head injuries and stab wounds, one in the genital area indicating that a blade had been inserted vertically. She worked as an entertainer in Japan.

> Could it be in 40 floors of windows, rooms
> beds and kitchen sinks is where
> you once laughed saying this arm will pay for
> Dodoy's next semester at school
> this leg for Christena's girl scout uniform.
> Arms scrubbing bathrooms all day
> legs walking endless streets in the afternoons
> to find ama's particular herb
> ANGAT SA BUHAY, ANGAT SA BUHAY
> *Life will get better,* you would say.
> *It will all happen …*
> I would add at once, *Once we return!*
> and we would both laugh.
>
> Singaporean prisons are spartan but humane.

*MARGIE MILITANTE: died on April 17, 1992, allegedly of cardiovascular arrest. Her body bore stab wounds in the stomach, contusions on the knees, feet and head, and her left arm was broken. She was a domestic worker in Riyahd, Kingdom of Saudi Arabia.

> I remember what had been written:
> *"*Kailangang masipag*
> *at matatag ka sa trabaho.*
> *Maging matatag ang kalooban*
> *at huwag makalimot sa Diyos."*
> ("Be industrious and persevering
> in your work, be strong-willed,
> and don't forget God.")
> Crying is sometimes the cause
> of quarrels between Filipina domestic helpers
> and their employers … you see,
> shedding tears brings
> bad luck to a family.
> Employers sigh:
> *"What shall I do with my Filipino maid? …*
> *She cries in the morning, she cries at noon,*
> *She cries in the afternoon, she cries in the evening,*
> *and she cries before going to sleep.*
> *I am getting concerned because*
> *our business is having difficulties."*
> Maybe because they're lonely,
> maybe that's why they cry.

*Then*
... they always ask ...
*why did they come?*

Singaporean prisons are spartan but humane.

*FLOR CONTEMPLACION: death by hanging, order of the Singaporean government for the murder of Delia Maga and her ward Nicholas Huang. The Singaporean findings state that Delia was strangled to death with an elastic cord, and Nicholas, the young boy she was taking care of, died from drowning in a pail full of water, head down. A second autopsy done by the Philippine government points out that Delia Maga had a big crack on her skull, a broken left shoulder, a battered spine, and four fractured ribs. These findings were not in the Singaporean reports.

Could it be that in this place
I saw you and forgot
we were in here together, friends.
Could it be that in this place
I wound that cord around your neck,
made your tongue ball like meats
you find hanging and sold in palengkes.
It is almost hideous, but what has been done
is a tongue for a tongue.
We will see, we will wait,
resilient hands that wash clothes,
feet that lead baby carriages,
and eyes that watch children wait.
Graves can be exhumed, files opened.

Singaporean prisons are spartan but humane.

\*Source: *LAYA Quarterly* and *Solidarity Journal*

# Edge of the Archipelago

I.

What Korina knew about
where she came from
included configurations
of numbers and symbols
situating a municipality in the northwestern corridor of a region
where she spent
her first month of life.

Malangas
07° 37'N
123° 02'E

Malangas
Zip Code: 7038

What Korina knew about
where she came from
included facts and geodetic surveys
identifying people she did not grow up with
and fertile municipalities and towns she will never visit.

Malangas
28,916 total population
28,786 households
21,483 Catholics

Malangas
Margo sa Tubig, Guipas, Siay

Malangas
Natural Resources include gold, copper, chromite, coal, iron, manganese, lead, clay, agricultural lands, forests

What Korina knew about
where she came from would visit her during desolate moments
in between dreams.
Imagining an irregular coastline
12,648 kilometers away
she would then wonder
how similar or how different could it be
from the coastline of California where she was raised.

II.

In 1919,
US army engineers came.
Eusebio Suyco was proud
of being the "only dark-skinned" native
allowed to wear the same cap
all the tall American army men wore.
He was one of 5 dark-skinned men
asked to join them in their excursions
to develop their town's mines.

Sent to determine boundaries.
Sent to determine property lines.

Men by the hundreds building
railroads for the Malangas coalmines.
Eusebio in his later years often talked of Conrado,
one of the many Cebuanos who never returned home
after the malaria scare hit camp.
He was the particular one
terrified and needed a hand to hold
when he urinated
because blackwater fever
made him pass urine
the same color as the coal
being mined for the Americans.
With his limbs shaking and teeth chattering
he would repeat what his wife told him
the last few weeks before he left Cebu:
*Don't leave me to work so far away!*
*She must have known.*
*She must have known.*
He believed
that the coal from underground
had seeped through his body
and finally
how this must have been God's way
of cleansing him
before giving him passage into his kingdom
for his past was one of drinking and gambling.

Between seizures and hot spells
he would call out the names of his sons:
*Aquilino! Clodoveo! Mariano!*

Conrado refused a quiet death
and caused sleepless nights
for an American
stationed next to his tent.
Distressed by the unrelenting tropical heat
and Conrado's cries,
he would later write
back to his wife
that malaria turned men into animals
and how the one
housed next to him

sounded like the red wolves
he remembered wandering the rivers of North Carolina.

Eusebio watched over Conrado for five long days,
made sure his final wages
were sent back to Cebu
along with his wedding band
and the black leather belt
bartered from the Americans.
Upon his return from the coal mines,
it would have been
a gift for his eldest son.

III.

Dirk Filmore always repeated the same story in memorials each year to Filipino war veterans that when the Japanese attacked Pearl Harbor on December 7, 1941, the cargo carrier he was in, the USS GOLD STAR, part of the Asiatic Fleet, was coaling at Malangas, Zamboanga.

The US Naval Code Word for this place was BASALT.

IV.

The people
from this place
who share Islam are at war right now.

Tied to geography and the land
the people of the flooded plains
the people living around the lake
the people of the current
Maguindanaons, Maranaos, Tausogs

V.

This place has a high-grade coal reserve
a heating value of 12,000 BTU
the highest coal grade that can be mined in the country.
The Philippine government have big economic interests in this region
and have stepped up the Armed Forces of the Philippines presence in
the region to neutralize the Bangsa Moro resistance.

VI.

Mohamad's weekly letters to Hadjid living in Sabah
spoke of his growing fear that he was "next."
*The anti-moro campaign has resumed …*
It is the 70's all over again
*… just worse. I will be following you to Malaysia in a few weeks.*
Hadjid knew his cousin
should have covered his face and
run from the journalists and their cameras
that were at the Malangas March for Peace.
Days later
Mohamad was shot dead while riding
his motorcycle in the middle of the town square.
His cousin was with him.
His cousin got away.
He is now hidden somewhere in the city safe.

VII.

Korina was told that once there was confusion
about this region's true name.
She liked both but preferred
the Samal's word *samboangan* or "mooring place"
over the Subanon's word *jambangan* for "land of flowers."
She later found out it was all a matter of translation and geography.
For the Subanons made their homes in interior highlands
abundant with flowers
while the Samals and other Muslims
lived on the coast and river mouths.

She has further data compiled in her dreams
about this place.
About this place
that anchors her lineage
to stories and histories that may
or may not have ever happened.

CLEARANCE
EALTH SERVICE
NE DIVISION

l of the U. S. Public Health Service.

CHOLERA
U. S. PUBLIC H
QUARANTI

No. BL529

Port of departure: MANILA
Name of ship: E/ROSSIA
Date of departure: July 16, 1926
Last permanent residence:
82 LEGASPI, W.C. MANI
Name of Passenger:
IGNACIO VALDEZ
Examined and found Bacteriologically negative
for cholera at: MANILA
Date: July 16, 1926

Surgeon, U. S. P. H. S.

Not valid unless impressed with seal

# Reclamation

> *Memory is an archipelago of closed-view*
> *coffins, eaten calmly like sugared*
> *fingers of bread.*
> —R. Zamora Linmark, *Rolling the R's*

# Abaca Queen and Battery "Murphy" and a Mariveles Moonlit Night

For in honor of this man that left in 1945,

I refuse that Battery "Murphy" was one of those poor boys
who had nothing better to do but enlist.
I refuse a hometown in Iowa or North Dakota or Nebraska.
I refuse boys on furlough, *putang ina's* and one-night stands.
I refuse lovemaking in background of mortar fire
    in fear that tomorrow meant a shell rooting itself
    deep in your gut.

For one night in Mariveles harbor,

Douglas Murphy USA S852251
in service for the sake of glory
called New York or San Francisco or Boston home
discovered a girl with rough hands from the abaca field
and loved this tropical queen
in a warm, glorious night, cease-fire observed
and created
the abaca princess
Erene Murphy
in all her splendor.

## Zamboangeña Exoticas

My name is Renee Brown
daughter of the town prostitute
of Zamboanga, Erene Brown.

Erene Brown was a GI baby
daughter of a white man in soldier's uniform
who gave her light brown hair and eyes
nothing more.
Renee Brown was a bastard baby
daughter of a brown man in policeman's uniform
who gave her dark brown hair and eyes
nothing more.

It is so odd that most probably
in a night of exotica meets GI Joe
a child was not meant to be conceived
and still
out
slithered
my
mother
Erene Brown.
It is so odd that most probably
in a night of exotica meets married man in policeman's uniform
a child was not meant to be conceived
and still
out
slithered
my body
Renee Brown.

I sometimes get jealous of this town prostitute
created under the throes of passion and war.

For I,
Renee Brown
was created by a need for money.
An amount
enough
to buy one
kilo
of
dark
carabao
meat.

## Papa's Back

Ties strewn on the floor,
a quick kiss ... Papa's back.
His tattered boarding pass
falls on the floor
as he opens his wallet
and takes out foreign bills
he did not use.
Something glitters on top
of his suitcase — a new golden watch
for Mama. She listens:
*Japan was hectic ... meetings*
*til midnight ... it's really expensive there.*
I crouch under his busy arms
but he stands
up,
reaches for a
shiny box,
*For you,* he says.
I stare as he opens it.
A pretty doll, this one with
a silk kimono.

I look up,
He's already
on the other
side
of the room
hanging a wrinkled suit.
*Meetings til midnight and the hotels ...*
Hugging my new doll
facing
Papa's back.

# Nene

—When was the last time you saw me?*

*The last time my husband saw me was the day Antoinette's nose bled from lack of sleep. She was crying all morning about the books and pictures she would have to leave behind. He wore the suit we bought in Cartimar, the same one he wore months back when we took our last family portraits. I wore a matching colored skirt, a type of woolen material too hot for Manila weather. But I had anticipated the colder weather I was arriving to.*

*This was also the same day, after good-byes and hugs and promises to call-once-we-got there, our son wouldn't leave his bedroom, hoping that when night time passed, he would wake to Antoinette's voice yelling at the neighbor's dog out in the street. All this according to a letter the maids sent me months later.*

*That was the very last time he saw me.*

—Was I the same then as I am now? How did I wear my hair? I'm sure you won't remember.*

*I had forgotten. I think my hair was short. The sunspots filling my face were freckles back then. My fingers wider, he notices the wedding ring he gave me was now something decorative for our daughter to wear. Back then, I was worried about the jewelry I had to leave behind, quick to remind him to bring them once they could follow.*

*Before we walked through the departure area entrance, the last thing I whispered in his ear was a reminder to pay the charges sent by the Waa Boarding House for the month that I stayed there. Our children thought I had gone away to visit my parents in Cebu. Before the move to Los Angeles, they didn't notice that we weren't spending time together.*

—People have to remember what really happened, not the lies.*

—So far it's all true, I'm sure of that.*

*questions Maria da Gloria asked her lover Josemar in Manuel Puig's novel *Blood of Requited Love*

# Antoinette

The month before my sister left Los Angeles to
move to Madrid, she told me about how people
in train stations began to infiltrate her dreams
once more.

The last time I heard her talk of it was age 11,
the summer
she and our mother
left for their move to the United States.
She had spent her last evening in Manila
sorting through 30 family albums, given a
directive
to take only one for her trip.
She took the album filled with pictures of the
women in our family.

A quick promise was made by our father that
the rest of the albums would be sent by boat at
a later time.
They never came.

On the way to the airport she had finally fallen
asleep in the car, then woke with a start and
said:
*People we knew were in this one, Frederick.*
*'Mi was there.*
With the mention of our grandmother,
her voice dropped to an even lower pitch:

*She was walking on top of a moving train trying to*
*maintain her balance using a little Japanese parasol.*
*With the strong motion of the train and her old age,*
*she slipped and hit the side of the tracks, falling*
*to the ground. At once, the train disappeared and*
*suddenly our surroundings lost color and we were in*
*a room of gray. 'Mi's five daughters suddenly appeared,*
*frozen, looking on with rage. I had been the only one to*
*run to her, grab her and hold her in my arms. I then*
*noticed how her body had shrunk but more frighteningly,*
*how soft it had become. She still had her shape but it*
*was as if all her bones had disintegrated under her*
*skin. I hugged her even tighter to stop what I couldn't*
*explain was happening. She flattened, and all that*
*was left was skin.*
All of the women stood around her – daughters.
It seemed like there were thousands of them
looking and glaring.

From then on,
women ceased appearing in her dreams.

## Dear Emanuella

I want you near the ocean's edge
standing as I write this love
letter to you thousands of miles
away, mother.

I've carried in me the weight of
your confusion and longing
to have a man carry you in their palm.
Each movement revealing your vigilance
for signals that a man was once
again leaving.

I do the same thing
a generation later.
The names are different
but it's all the same—
the feel of a man's palm
sliding down my back,
the chime of a promise uttered
and the utter grief
of their departure
from our beds.
All these hurts
dig inside our hearts.

Many do not know that I
have never seen your face
and all I can do is try
to see you in mine.

Every time I grieve and think
there is no way to go on,
I reach for a feeling
only you could have passed on to me.
Always losing it and searching for
this particular feeling in various
rooms and cars,
trying to contain it
not let it slip away.

This morning I thought
of something new.
I will walk away from the ocean's edge
and fill my pockets with sand.
I wonder, mother, if this weight I carry
will be enough
to fill the decades of loss between us.
Let the sand fill your heart,
make me light once again
so I can walk in different towns
and countries
traverse deserts
and lie in green forests
sleep soundly for
one night
and feel my shoulders
fall.

For one night let the sand
fill us up
so we can finally sleep.

# Scattered Cities

> *There's really no such thing as the "voiceless."*
> *There are only the deliberately silenced,*
> *or the preferably unheard.*
> — Arundhati Roy

## A London Adolescence

Through St. Alban's Grove
she began how father
would not leave
her alone.
Through the left turn by
Gloucester Road,
she told me about his
hands and how
they would
not leave
her alone.
Through Brompton Court
she told me about
bleeding in her
own bed.
Then finally Imperial Way
age 14 and she wishes
she were dying.

She walked through her front door
as I tried to gather each word
that spilled into these streets.
These words are to hang in front
of the house for everyone to see.

## Staircases

Zarah,
It is a year later
and I still remember
the talks through
cigarette smoke
in staircases
about willful fathers
and virginity.
    Arguments
    til early morning
    with Ibrahim,
    Sa-id, Mahmut
    and Tel-al.
    They would not stop
    until they thought
    they had
    won.
        You had a
        fascination with
        darkness, firecrackers,
        one's soul
        and cypress trees.
        In discussions
        about broken hymens
        with next day repairs,
        you would say
        *Do not laugh, it is true.*
            I remember a passion
            for Gibran and the
            poetry you wrote
            that rumbled
            read in Arabic.
                I was told that
                you've left those smoky
                staircases
                and have gone back
                to willful fathers,
                cypress trees
                and darkness.
                    Until we find
                    the time to once
                    more sit in those
                    smoky staircases,
                    do not let rambling
                    sparks with colors
                    red, white and blue
                    find you.
                    In the bottom of those
                    staircases I will wait.

# A Virgin Sings Her Song

Next day repairs
not like a car, not with glue.
Deep in the heart of Arab life
there are certain London roads
where next day repairs
go on
not like a car, not with glue
but with needles and hymen
sewn to perfection once more.
My Jordanian lover accepting of
the new woman he gets every time.
He will not marry me
but pays for such repairs:

*It is the 20th century.*
*Oh how far we've come!*

Spending pounds and pounds
prices go up and down.
I feel like a car in need
of a tune-up, dear doctor
in blue, smiles and says:

*We're losing so much, my*
*dear. I will have nothing*
*to sew back up pretty soon.*

Next day repairs, next day
repairs, yes, now like a
car assembled with glue.
My Jordanian lover has
left me to marry a virgin.

I had been a frequent visitor
of certain London roads
now left with my
stitches, hymen,
and nothing else,
stitches and hymen
yes, nothing else.

# Sons

Yesterday
Beppe found out
that he would be a father.
*It will be a son.*
*It will be a son.*
Proud in bringing
his offering to
the world.

Yet
does he know,
daughters from far away
are drowned in
marshy fields by
Mother hands?
Daughters' feet
are bound and
mangled beyond
repair by
Grandmother skills?
Daughters far away
sit in dark rooms
awaiting cleansing
of mind
of body
in Sister chairs?

Aside from this.
Aside from this.
Aside from this.
Tomorrow
Beppe will walk along Via Marsala
shouting proud
as his father did
for him.

As he has been taught:
It is
always
better
to
start
a family
with a
son.

# In Finding Père Lachaise

> *Life is a gift*
> *from the few to the many*
> *from those who know and who have*
> *to those who know not and have not.*
> — Amedeo Modigliani

Dedo,
I didn't walk through rue Caulaincort—
Paris is too big to grant me the pleasure.
In the Boulevard du Montparnasse
a man stops to ask time.
I say I don't speak French.
He is delighted and asks my purpose.
He confuses English with French with English,
not realizing I don't care for his conversation.
I am tired as
I break his fast speech
and ask for
Rue
Caulaincort— *the old studio,* and then
add your name.
He says he knows of a better place to find you.

The true bohemian;
The vagabond par excellence.
Dedo,
It does not show,
It does not echo here.
Père Lachaise Cimetière
does not give this impression of you.

Self-indulgence for those who didn't know; for you
meant being alive.
Excess for those who didn't have; for you
meant possessing the key to the celebrated spirit of painting.
A passionate cellist.
A youthful girl with braids.
Women with blank eyes
and tilted heads.

"Death took him at the moment he achieved glory."
Those who didn't know have imprinted on your headstone
an incorrect epitaph.

# A New Way of Seeing Things

I.

He's got his list of ingredients ready you know.
It's going to be different this year.
He hands over a drink recipe
and it's the same one handwritten on a notecard
laminated for long wear
for what he thinks he'll be carrying
for the rest of his life.

A recipe for a new life
he hands to a bartender:
12 ounces ginger ale, chilled
3 cups pineapple juice, chilled
8 1/2 ounces cream of coconut
along with a sad smile hoping
she will place
an umbrella leaning to the left,
make it look like a real drink
in an unreal place
one that he's been told
he should never go back to again.
Others wouldn't understand, you know.
They will undoubtedly say
*What's wrong with you,*
*Where's the spirited boy we've always known?*

II.

—I left him crouched inside a beat up '76 Honda
on a 53 degree Fahrenheit Thanksgiving night
just having eaten a minimart hotdog with some apple juice.
—I left him crouched in a chain bookstore
waiting for a familiar face
patrolling the self-help section to find out
why success has always eluded him.
—I left him crouched in dark rooms,
3-second sparks
and 34-hour sleep daze.

III.

12 ounces ginger ale, chilled
3 cups pineapple juice, chilled
8 1/2 ounces cream of coconut
make it look like a real drink
it's still important.

# Dear Martin

We visited you today
for the last time.
I looked around
this last city you lived in
cross-referencing what you said in calls made mid-mornings:
*There's nothing around here*
*I'm in the middle of*
*nowhere*
*I miss*
*LA*

Ella plays on a car radio.
As I drove nearer to the address written with pencil on yellow paper
I entered the landscape you created
four walls that squeezed your brain and your heart.

Blue and brown, sky and earth.
Buildings to move into for just $1.
Banners that promise coming home to serenity.
This place where the rocks jut out
the side of mountains.
Gravel roadways, adobe colors
away from the center of squalor
casinos, dancing girls and alcohol in the streets.

I see a three-year-old boy waiting
for you to walk in the door
for his oatmeal and guitar lesson.
I see a sixteen-year-old girl waiting
for a quick conversation
about music, money and fame.
The woman you left and her two
children sitting by the couch
pass around pictures of you
taken one, two, three months back?

It doesn't look like you, Martin.
All I could do is think
how you would have enjoyed this sunny day.

## Breathe (the capitalist whirr)

I see you, lady,
crouching behind
the cash register with your
worried face.
You remind me that
I too sit behind a desk
but with my back straight
vision locked to
a computer screen
staring at letters and numbers
that hold no importance for me.
What my superior does not see
when she turns her head back
is the secret I protect
inside the middle of my stomach.
Unrevealed, the weight of it
makes me crouch just like you.
We spend hours in rooms
where we are told
what rules are in place.
Smiles we paste everyday are
a momentary nicety that
keeps all secrets safe.

I want to share with you
this secret I keep in my belly,
the one I tell my animals
when I get home each night:
*It is like being strangled
and the last ounce of air left inside
your chest being choked
out slowly, slowly
tight and tighter then always
quickly released.*
This.
Repeated a thousand times a day,
no one allowed respite or exit.
These cubicles
like little torture chambers
reshaped from another era
now refashioned nightmares.

*But still, but still
we dream of
oxygen tanks by the thousands.*

# A Rat Got Out

I.

Sometimes when the office is quiet
I hear shuffling.
It's like a slow ink jet printer
on its last legs
printing the last page of a very long document.
I stop what I'm doing and I listen some more.
Sometimes it's pounding hammers
like small construction sites
in the room next to me.
What do we tell ourselves everyday?
It's just plastic boxes and mazes that hold little foot paws
that wait, scurry, wait, eat, wait, drink and die.

II.

There was a tizzy the other month
when a big rat was found running through the halls.
It tried to make its way through the office break room.
Memos were sent;
staff people disgusted.
Memos were sent;
kitchen sanitized.
Memos were sent;
traps were set for the dirty rodent.
All everyone could think about for weeks was that rat
probably hungry making a break for it.

III.

It was one of the uninitiated rats living outside and wanting to get in.
It was one of the ones who didn't know any better and believed the tales passed
down by other rats of what life might have been like inside this building where
cool air ran through laboratory hallways at all times and gave
refuge from all they ever knew — the heat of machines and dry rotting fruits.

IV.

This is what I tell myself everyday.
He escaped and will reveal
the lies about our comfortable temperatured rooms.

V.

*Coats, white and blue*
*smiling faces with clean-smelling hands*
*windows covered with thick white paper.*
*He must have seen that small hind paw*
*cut and discarded.*
*He must have seen it*
*fall off a plate forever lost*
*in a side slot between a steel table*
*and a formica desk.*

VI.

The cool air is a trap ... so many of them die in there.

# The Small-Town Dictator

*for Kian Loyd delos Santos*

*What about that small-town dictator from the hinterlands*
*who tried to find ways to rope his prisoners just the right way,*
*delighted in seeing them suspended high in midair*
*just taut enough to make them squeal like*
*the slaughtered pigs he heard outside his window*
*every Thursday night?*

And then your reply:
-he was a murderer, a psychopath, a special case
I add:
-he wasn't actually the one who roped the
prisoners or pulled them up to hang
-what of the men he paid to do it?

All done to get that regular flow of pesos
to purchase the pencils, cell phones, and uniforms
needed by their families.
These men learned to numb their insides,
put wax inside their ears to drown out the sounds,
and eucalyptus oil under their nose to counter the smell
of urine, blood, and feces that ended up on their slippers.
They were the small murderers.
The big murderer wore white and never got soiled.

A dictator's secretary hums this song nightly to his little children:
*We are just one cruel act away towards each other.*
*If we can easily do it to an animal,*
*we are but one animal away from doing it to each other.*

# Smog

> *Though we tremble before uncertain futures*
> *may we meet illness, death and adversity with strength*
> *may we dance in the face of our fears.*
> —Gloria E. Anzaldúa

# Months

*for Napoleon Lustre*

I.

Essex said it perfect:
*It is easier to be furious than yearning.*
You belong to tribes of warriors and outlaws.
Many who are now dying or just waiting like you.
As I sit here by your bed looking at your sleeping body,
I wonder how long your fury can sustain you.

II.

This is a love song to a friend
whose remaining time with me
is determined by facts and figures
from studies, accounts, tests.
*Many have lived over 10 years since diagnosis.*
My friend, it is your tenth year
and you are getting sick
so much more frequently now.
I am finding out that nobody really knows.

III.

As I drive these freeways and reach the golden hour
I will remember you and what I said about the beautiful color
this time of day gives the earth.
*Healthy, vibrant and new.*
It would hit your dark skin and make you golden,
healthy, vibrant and new.
If I could only make you healthy, vibrant and new
with these words, I would.
I remember afternoons in your room over
Italian Roast and Benson & Hedges
and talk of cinema and discussions
about the fascinating curl of your spine.

IV.

You are brown, like me
coming from tropical islands we both
dream of going back to.
Do you know that after
leaving you each time
to go home to
my own life,
I am reminded of typhoon season
and the green spread of luscious cogon
in the mountains of Badian?
You bring me back
and for this exile
lonely and wanting of things familiar
you give me sustenance.

V.

I look at your hands and see monkey hands.
I look at your arms and see how thin they have become.
I see you from across a crowded room and see your dark brown skin.
I see you dance and know we may never be able to do this again.

VI.

You were born somewhere else, not here
not in this country where you found the gay ghetto.
Eleven years ago
you were somebody else.
When I asked your mama,
*What did he lose?*
she wailed,
*His life! His life!*
You are scared that she will see you die,
I am scared that I will see both of you die.

VII.

I dreamt of you a long time ago —
in my dream you weren't as you are now.
You inhabited different shapes
and wore different masks
but you were there with that stare
and presence that told me
*You are not alone.*
*I am here and will always be here.*
I am scared of growing old and not being able to tell you
I love you everyday.
I have to remind myself that when you are gone,
what that woman said
about you leaving your mark on her skin forever.
You are in blood, bone, and marrow.

## One of the Worst Days

He said:
*These are the ravages of a sickly body.*
I countered:
*These are the ravages of a mind that has given up.*
He looked up, smiled a bit.
*You don't know, girl.*
*I've been fighting this for eleven years.*
I left him alone and asked myself,
how do you keep one afloat from
battle fatigue
if all you can offer are words?
He wants a new body or no body at all.
With a puff from his cigarette, he said slowly:
*There is ceasefire in most battles,*
*you know, come sit and rest with me.*
I offered one last word ... hope ...
He smiled at me:
*That will do for now.*
I grabbed the word to have it envelope us like a shield.

# Rock/Adept/Water

*for Peter*

There is a Chinese movie you remind me of:
first shot is water
falls,
a man seeking repair for broken dreams and
longing for what cannot be.
Payphones and distance from fathers who
do not care why calls are made
and where they are calling from.

There is a book I found behind a rock that told me
your secrets:
what your mother said the last day you were together,
the name of an old lover who still lives in your dreams,
the color of your grandfather's favorite coat, the one he wore the winter of his death.

There is a certain way to hear
your imagination's language:
make friends with a minor note that hides in city dwelling pianos,
have coffee with various fingertips that leave their owners' mark on bass guitars,
kiss errant dogs who find the bend of a chain-link fence ...
All these make me adept at sensing the tension that manifests in your brow.

## Let Me Tell You

I have heard it already, baby.
This could be about how your skin tastes like mango
and how I will lose myself in your 'Pinas skin.
I could bring up pride in your homegirl talk
and fierceness with your Carson homeboys
who say
*you're fine, girl*
and still call other women
*my bitch.*
But baby, instead this is what I want to tell you.

Come near me and let me smell your skin
wipe the sweat that drips from the front of your
neck to the curve of your left
breast with my palm
in this sweat-soaked bed.

As I see you spread out in this dark room
I will light a hundred candles to illuminate
this night, take those
arms lying on your side
lick your
wrists, guide them through my
back, slowly kiss your
left ear and whisper this:
*dinhi, karun* – here, now.
I want to graze the tips of your
breasts with my fingers, feel their shape
with the back of my hand.

Candle lights will flicker around this room and your long
black hair will serve as
the night sky I have seen countless times, dreaming of Malangas.
As my hands pencil the shape of your
hips, your ass,
as my hands slowly caress the inside of your
thighs, my head will move down and rest upon your
lower stomach, and my
tongue will stay between your legs.

Standing inches away
I lean you against this wall
my left hand clasping both your
hands hidden behind your waist.
Let me find on the side of your
neck, the taste of this evening's
humidity
conversation
and
laughter.
Leave nationhood
family
love in a different place

away
from this
brightly lit room.

Come near me
*dinhi, karun*
come near me
and let me start all this with a kiss.

# To a White Woman in the Greyhound Station, Sacramento

The latest is what's mama to do about
removing the strawberry stain Maniya
got from the party. Then there is
Renzo who worries that the new girl
he likes will find out that he
doesn't own a car. Papa is scared
they may think he is too old and
they will make him retire. I
worry about acne and what it will
do to my complexion.

These worries cloud your own living rooms and houses.

## Los Angeles Pilipinas

Let me tell you about Los Angeles Pilipinas
City of Angels pinays ... some born here, others back home.


I.

Corezi Ramirez
takes 5 minimum punches on her face
by the cheekbones.
Binugbog Queen they call her
15 years living by Rampart & Temple
4 kids alongside a husband with a candied tongue
a type of sweetness that manifests
itself with greenish blue markings
on pretty brown skin.

II.

Irma Illustre
martyr extraordinario
novena every morning at 5
angelus in the afternoon
Sunday masses without fail
to pray for a son's soul
shot
by another friend's son
in a night of yosi, hoochis, serbesas.
Just a get-together
party party?

III.

Her daughter
Jing Illustre
Cal State LA'er sana for the Fall of '92
downhill a few months before from an incident
with a nobyo who refused to understand
HUWAG!
AYOKO!
'Don't want to's' turned into
a pretty brown baby boy
who now carries the Illustre name
not his father's name.

IV.

Chona Sevilla
hides the fact that welfare checks feed
a son, a daughter.
She takes the bus
going on long treks
carrying heavy bags
you see.
She goes to another part of town

so no one will see
yung mga binabayaran niya
the things she pays for
are compliments of the US government.

V.

Belen Antoinette
T-bird totoo.
She married a man
she didn't love to please familia.
They own big businesses
successful of course.
Bahay in the Los Feliz Hills.
Friday nights, while her husband
is paying a puta on Sunset Boulevard
she is dancing to her heart's
content over at Girl Bar
Lesbian Bar
Tibo Bar.
There she finds love.

VI.

Maricar Cunanan
has a view of Malibu Beach
sees Catalina on a clear day and
on certain days
the hand of her puti boss under her skirt.
She watches over his 3 beautiful children and cooks for his wife.
She says: There's no such thing as low-class maids in the USA
Degree in Accounting from UST
Here: au pair, nanny.

VII.

Chinggay Manalastas is tough girl from Belmont High.
Believed in pinay brown, pinay power
which gave her the attitude to withstand
being followed in the Glendale Galleria
rude service banda Orange County.
Trying hard to hold on
to that attitude
after an initiation process brought
about by brown men
who supposedly believed
in pinay power.
Viva the brown woman kuno.
Gang raped, she has dropped out of high school.

VIII.

Nerissa X.
Her permanent address is Skid Row
sa Downtown.
Yes, there is a Pilipina

there
downing a bottle of gin and
an occasional piping of crack.
Left by her pen pal
drug addict husband
5 years ago.
No family here
no family back home.
This mail-order bride
has found her Tondo in the new world.

IX.

Rosas Ysiquia. Thank God nalang
for health insurance.
HIV+ 6 months ago
full blown AIDS today.
Unprotected lovemaking one
night from a guapo in Bayanihan Restaurant.
He is now gone, she is lying alone at Queen of Angels Hospital.


Let me tell you about Los Angeles Pilipinas.
Some are dying inside for a brush of a familiar
tropical breeze they remember.
Some driving along a freeway smiling
thanking fortune for Medicare
future social security checks
Fedco membership cards.

# Off Rampart

I.

This is a moment she needs.
The dry air telling her that once again it is season to wash your face in the morning
afternoon
and night.
She misses the humidity of *Mandaue* now in this place
this street
this alley
this place that had not welcomed any of them from the start.

II.

This is not the weather she arrived to — *United Stets*.
Then was a November
bright
sweet.
Eternal Novembers in the many
"when I first came to this country" essays
she had written every year til 6th grade at Rosemont Elementary.

III.

With sunken bones and stilted English
she took a second look at him
wanting to forgive him
for beating her mother.
This father who was a mechanic
this father who was a tile layer
and sometimes the father
who did nothing but stare out a window
in the corner of the house
looking for more than
this corner plot
corner street.

IV.

The daughter is home again.
He does not know that she
dances naked before countless men
soaps their backs and feeds them with
her *oohs* and *ahhs,*
in her head
conversations with non-men:
*How interesting life must be.*
When she goes home she changes the color of her nails
different colors after different men
lining up the bottles against her window sill.
She talks about creating those smart-looking
broken glass floors she had seen in mansions and
private rooms.
From these crushed

65

manicure bottles
mixtures of sienna, azure, cool lime.
How bright the broken patterns would look.
Different colors for different days
different men
different angles
forming a walkway
leading to the back door that
opens into an alley
*Bento Wey* the old men in the corner call it.

V.

There is a picture of a white waitress
from the now gone 6th Street Sambo's eatery in his dresser.
He is smiling beside her holding a menu.
Two seconds before the picture was taken
she had looked at him
curiously
after
a comment he made:
*It is so interesting that you are serving me,*
*I am in America!*

# A Second Sky

I.

There are approximately 7,337 miles
of land & sea between Manila and Los Angeles.

II.

Starting in the 70's, different years
marked different arrivals. Mid-70's
the mother came, early 80's the
daughter came while the brother and
the father arrived in the late 90's.

III.

In the 80's, the daughter was 11, a
darker skinned, black haired, brown
eyed girl coming to the land of blue
eyed, blonde, beautiful valley girls.
The city of stars and Hollywood.

IV.

It is now the 90's, the son has
acclimated well, but retirement here in
the US holds a different story for the
father, now in his late sixties, held
back by advanced emphysema. The
son now only talks of how different it
would have been if his father had
come earlier.

V.

*What I miss most about the Philippines are
my friends, I never had a dull moment there.
I frequently would meet with my friends in
bars. Anywhere I would go there was always
somebody I would meet that I knew.*

VI.

*My wife knowing my inclination for pets was
suggesting that I set up a marine or
freshwater aquarium here. Knowing what it
took to maintain an aquarium in the
Philippines, I just would not do it. It is not
easy to maintain a marine aquarium. Yes,
you can maintain it by way of artificial water
but the corals and the fishes do not survive
that well with artificial salt water.
In the Philippines I did use fresh sea water
for my aquariums.*

VII.

There, in their condo now in Glendale no pets are allowed. Nothing, zilch.

VIII.

*I don't know if they'll even allow us to probably have a little bird. (small laugh) An aquarium I would assume should be allowed because it's not a nuisance to the neighbors. But the rule is hard and fast on that. Too bad, maybe better for me because as I said, it's not easy to maintain an aquarium.*

uneasy

there was an uneasy air between the two of us
the way we walked around the room
and how suddenly days and nights went by too fast
all our conversations revolved around time.
as soon as he would turn off the tv
i would turn on the radio.
there was a silence we would not allow
in the room
for it would only allow us to think
and remember what could be taken away.
silence would open up a hole in the universe
where life could escape.
shuffling sounds from our footsteps
father's noisy gurgling breathing
mother's fingers hitting the plastic-covered remote control
each sound embraced for the space it filled.

# Frederick

After living two years in the new country, my brother took to drinking to find "spirits." He keeps to 7 bottles of beer every afternoon and at 5 p.m., gets in his car, listens to Sinatra and heads towards downtown LA. He knows that at a precisely calculated driving speed, the blur of trees and railroad tracks along San Fernando Boulevard and Avenue 19 outside his car window will remind him of "home." A blur resembling the busy streets of *Reposo* and *Kalayaan,* quiet now that the night ladies have found their customers for the evening and all that is left are quiet roads with stunted, *jeepney* exhaust-blackened trees lining the narrow sidewalks.

He knows that at just the right volume, his tape of 40's Sinatra will sound like it did years back in his father's automobile, on their way home from a weekly visit with uncles and cousins and then remember that on certain stop lights, his father would give away a few centavos to make a young beggar girl pressing her mother or grandmother's face on the car window go away.

He knows at the right time of day, the golden hour when the sun falls on the buildings just right will make him remember how once again to feel whole, like how he used to be so long ago. He knows to stare beyond the tall, shiny buildings and put on his dark glasses because with just the right mix of shading, his eyes and spectacles can make the horizon glow in the same color of Manila smog and sky. This same color he saw for 16 years in the back window of our father's rented house before supper time.

Los Angeles is for him a city of memory where colors intensify and the small *Makati* creeks he used to play in become vast oceans he knows he will never return to.

# Lorena

I.

*There is this famous, older, white man unhappy and lives in the house I care for.*

II.

Kept in his service as the caretaker
as his caretaker for 15 years.
She has learned not to believe the face he presents
outside this house.
There are certain things only she is allowed to do.
Like opening him
a new bottle of dry sack sherry every evening.
She knows to use the glass
his oldest daughter bought him
from Kinsale.
Prepare Piazolla's 'rough dancer and the cyclical night'
in his record player.
Tango Apasionado plays til the sun
comes up the next morning.
He drinks mostly to mourn a dead lover
he lost 10 years ago.
He cries for him nightly and knows
he can do this in her company
after she once told him
*I come from a family with stories of our own.*

III.

These particular things he does not know:
-she started fainting when she arrived in this country
and now keeps faint pills in her left pocket
everywhere she goes
-she smells the insides of old phone books to find the
scent of humid Manila afternoons and damp marshes
only found behind abandoned cracked, red brick
school buildings
-she was born in the province of Ilocos Norte in a hut
you can still find standing beside the Laoag desert
dunes
-she writes letters home to grown children saying
*He is like me, looking for things we'll never find.*

IV.

In one of the many glass houses in Malibu there is a
woman who keeps safe the truths about this universe.

# Tata Dinong

I.

Tata Dinong passed his first summer in Los Angeles tending the plants in the second-floor veranda of the building where he lived. He spent his second and third winters outside his window listening, counting ambulances zooming down Temple Street. He frequently mentioned how the siren's flashing lights were the only kind of red his eyes allowed him to see. His eyes showed him the rest of the world a poor shade of gray and white.

II.

*I live in a bachelor apartment with 4 other old-timers like me. We avoid talking too much because the neighbor to our right is the brother of the apartment owner and if they knew how many bodies slept in this area of how many square feet? This $250 room is gone and will have us five old boys scrambling to find another cheap space.*

Nights back from work were done in pantomime fashioning a carefully mumbled nocturnal language only the five of them understood. They have evaded detection and have lived in the same building for ten years.

III.

Sunday mornings are spent in run-down fast food joints in downtown LA along with other men reminiscing about the second war and musical Glen Miller evenings and Artie Shaw afternoons after days of heavy mortar attack. *Malinta Tunnel, the Hayakawa Detachment, Mariveles Harbor, Camp O'Donnell,* names of something that was fought a long time ago. Someone brought a book he found in Goodwill, sharing it with the other men. This book only mentioned General MacArthur, Wainright, and how American soldiers always "held their line" during heavy artillery attack. All of them huddled in Formica chairs with 49 cent muffins and 39 cent coffees on top of Formica tables, he railed about how the battle in Corregidor was also fought by the men sitting with him. He made an oath to write a book of his own.

IV.

Conversations last fall were about the latest tips on how to avoid the morning rush in the county clinics, which nurses to flirt with to get a free flu shot on the side, SSI appeals and the best way to ask for more, recommendations like Crescent Church giving away free clothes, *Hiyas* market, the best place to get the best *bangus* and *tamatis*, SmileBrite by Rampart and

Temple taking patients with no dental insurance.
Cheap, cheaper, cheapest. Grocery cents off coupons
never used from the Sunday paper stack up and prop
the corner burner stove to make it stand even.

V.

Tata Dinong and the other four men had a mission
last month. Government checks were pooled along
with savings scraped from part-time jobs as security
guards in museums or perhaps doormen in the
various upscale residential hotels on the Westside.
With the collection added up, the conversion rate
from dollars to pesos presented itself a way to pay for a
wife's goiter operation in Zamboanga and books
and uniforms for a grandchild in the Barangay Diso
primary school and in return, pictures sent from
home fill an entire wall.

# Mar'

*after Nice Rodriguez*

I.

*"Proper girls are the most precious*
*things put on this earth*
*and proper girls need proper men,"*
was the last thing cousin Marita
would hear her father tell
her younger sister every night
before he sent them off to bed.
He always said goodnight to Mina
and would only give Marita a stern look.
He would say this to hurt her
but she knew the truth in it and
silently agreed
with what he said.
Communications were limited
to yells about skirts
she wouldn't wear
hair she wouldn't want braided
and ribbons and clips
she would throw out
the bus window on her way to school.
She was the second daughter
between the older and younger sister.
The middle daughter
who embarrassed her family
when she stole
a set of her uncle's briefs
when he came to visit from Australia.
He had the nice, imported kind,
the cotton blend that hugged her hips
and made her feel like a proper man.
Mar' was the neighborhood *tibo'*
who took on
an older brother's responsibility.
She took care of Mina,
befriending her suitors,
so she could find out
what kind of men they were.
*Proper girls should only go out with proper*
*men,* this she believed.
She observed what Mina's suitors did
in the company of other men:
how they gambled, drank and smoked.

They didn't mind her hanging around
because she was a *butch-ero*
and being seen with her announced to
the world that they were a favored group
eligible to court the *butch-ero's* sister
Miss Manila in last year's beauty pageant.

II.

Mar' avoided relationships
with common women
and kept her sights
on seeking the proper woman
not really knowing
what she was waiting for.
When her father kicked her
out of the house for refusing
to wear a dress to her mother's funeral
she knew it was time to move on
and went far to a new country
to leave everything and everyone
who didn't like her short hair and broad shoulders.

III.

With no word from her father
and dwindling phone calls from her
younger and older sisters
this *butch-ero* tried out
her life on her own.
Mar' found jobs in different restaurant bars
in East LA where they liked
her short hair and her manly gait.
She met a woman named Vianna at work
who wore the short, little skirts that Mar'
liked and had the long legs and deep
brown hair she desired.
Vianna was from Sao Paolo
and knew Mar' understood life
the way she did when
she caught her
sneaking out left-over food
from the restaurant kitchen.
Vianna had done the same thing.
They laughed at each other's secret find
and their giggling gave way
to regular late-night conversations
over coffee and cigarettes
in wonderment of the food that gets
thrown away in this new country
and how all of it could feed a whole town
a whole village back home.
This *butch-ero* was surprised
in discovering they both liked
the same shade of blue
colors that reminded them of skies
where they both came from.
Vianna was all Mar' had in this country
but that wasn't enough for Vianna
to stay on with her "proper man."
She left Mar' after 4 months
moving on to San Antonio, Texas.
This *butch-ero* cried

every night for six months.
She went out with other girls
wanting only to forget one
but not quite finding what she had lost.
After 9 months of this
one night
while playing Caetano Veloso
on a loop,
Mar' took out Vianna's favorite belt
which she had hidden in her closet
and hung herself
on a beam
in her bedroom.

IV.

None of us knew Mar' had left Manila to
move to California.
She had not called any of us
already living here.
We found out everything when the father and
oldest daughter traveled to Los Angeles
to take Mar's body back.
Her family had said that she was in
Riyadh, Saudi Arabia working in the
Dabi Oil Mining Company and doing well.

# Bing

I.

He has been in this city for 10 years
and all he would allow others
to know
for certain
about his life
is his love
for music of all kinds
but jazz preferably
and the accumulated number
of free poster calendars
he's collected
over the years
from every
Chinese-owned bakery and grocery
along Chinatown and
the Lincoln Heights periphery.

II.

The Mexican parking attendants
at work knew
that to get their weekends off
or be excused for being late to work
all they would have to do
was have Bing start talking about music.
Told him the title of a song
he had never come across.
Told him a musician's name
he had never heard of.
Then they could count on him
to become more
accommodating
and forgiving.
They talked among themselves
wondering if he perhaps
was once
a musician in the Philippines.
They all made sure
to go to the jazz section
of Ritmo Latino before work
or the weekend previous
to find a new musician's name or
Latin jazz band
to strengthen their case.
If they had not done
their homework,
they knew to ask
about one of the cassettes
Bing had in stacks of 6,
12 in each pile,
a total of 72 all in all:
They were inside
jewel cases
with masking-taped
identification tags.
Written
in faded ink:
*Koln 1978-8:00 PM, Distein 1977-4:40 PM*
*Arhus 1979-3:34 AM, Koln 1982-7:45 AM*

III.

When he was in the merchant marines,
Bing always had
a small cassette recorder
he brought with him
everywhere.
In every city he went to
he recorded music from the radio.
Serving as reminders
or evidence
of having been there
once or even twice.
He also has cassettes with music
from locations
like *Jansloo, Florida*
*Listra, California*
*Hina, Hawaii* and
*Sharks Edge, Alaska.*

IV.

He put up some
of his
favorite
smaller
poster calendars in the 3
narrow walls
that was his stall
in the underground parking area
of the tallest high-rise
in downtown Los Angeles.
He noticed
the trends
created
by the
promotional calendar industry.
From 1985-1990
12 different cities
from Europe each year.
Cities familiar
and unfamiliar to him
would grace his walls
at home and at work.
He had been to most
of these places
but May/88 Salzburg
was his favorite.
He made a promise
to buy himself
a cuckoo clock
and visit the biggest
opera hall the Viennese had built.

V.

After working years
parking luxury cars and vans
he got
his own little office
with a desk
and little TV.
Bing started bringing
the bigger calendars
to work.
His favorite
was the early 90's
when the calendar industry chose
to feature Asia.
He was
especially enamored
with the one he got
from the HoHo Fish Market
along Broadway,
for they were
the only ones
who had the kind
that featured all the cities
he had ever visited
before he moved to America.
This was also
the only calendar
that had 3 months in a row and
featured
each major city
from the
3 regions of the Philippines.

## VI.

He guards most importantly
the tapes with music
from cities named
Cebu
Manila
Zamboanga and
Davao.
These tapes are not part of the stacks
in his work desk.
These ones he keeps
in his workbag
brought to the office
the cigarette shop
the bakery 4 doors from his house
and even to church.
Each tape
he has listened to
at least for 5 minutes
from the day he arrived
and from then on,
each day he has lived in this city.

VII.

Each month that went
also meant
another ritual
of tearing each calendar page
and rolling it into bundles
to be put away in the broom closet
in his small apartment.
April 1991 – Region of Luzon
May 1991 – Region of the Visayas
June 1991 – Region of Mindanao
stayed on the wall
Bing faced every morning
when he came in to work.
What only changed
were the posters—
to his left
and to his right.
He would tell the men
working with him
about the best jazz joints
to go to
in Japan
Hong Kong
and Thailand.
They all knew
that they would have to
listen and just agree
even though
never in their wildest dreams
did they intend to make a trip
to any of the places he mentioned.
He always ended his tales
about each city
with a warning
to listen good!
*Who among you ever dreamed*
*you would be parking cars*
*in another country*
*or maybe like him*
*collect free calendars come December*

Lorena | *Eudocia\**
2001 | 2017

I.

| | |
|---|---|
| There is this famous, ~~older~~, ~~white~~ man unhappy and lives in the house I care for. | younger, Filipino American |

II.

| | |
|---|---|
| Kept in his service as the ~~caretaker~~ | Lola |
| as his ~~caretaker~~ for ~~15~~ years. | slave    52 |
| She has learned not to believe the face he presents outside this house. | |
| There are certain things ~~only she is allowed to do~~. | she couldn't stop doing |
| Like ~~opening him~~ | cooking breakfast |
| ~~a new bottle of dry sack sherry every evening.~~ | even when the whole family couldn't stay to eat. |
| She ~~knows to use the glass~~ | enjoyed making lavish meals |
| ~~his oldest daughter bought~~ him | and grinned with pleasure as the family |
| ~~from Kinsale~~. | devoured them. |
| ~~Prepare Piazolla's 'rough dancer and the cyclical night'~~ | Listening to |
| ~~in his record player.~~ | a cassette |
| ~~Tango Apasionado plays till the sun~~ | of Filipino folks songs |
| ~~comes up the next morning.~~ | the same tape over and over. |
| He ~~drinks mostly to mourn~~ a dead ~~lover~~ | writes and mourns, mother |
| he lost ~~10~~ years ago. | 12 |
| He cries for ~~him~~ nightly and knows | her |
| he can do this in ~~her~~ company | Lola's |
| after she once told him | |
| *I come from a family with stories of our own.* | |

III.

These particular things he does not know:

| | |
|---|---|
| ~~-she started fainting when she arrived in this country and now keeps faint pills in her left pocket everywhere she goes~~ | her childhood when and where she met Lieutenant Tom |
| ~~-she smells the insides of old phone books to find the scent of humid Manila afternoons and damp marshes only found behind abandoned cracked, red brick school buildings~~ | what her childhood crush Pedro looked like and why he left |
| -she was born in the province of ~~Ilocos Norte~~ in a hut you can still find standing beside the ~~Laoag desert dunes~~ | Tarlac Mayantoc hills |
| -she ~~writes letters~~ home ~~to grown children saying *He is like me, looking for things we'll never find.*~~ | sends money, for her siblings |

IV.

| | |
|---|---|
| In ~~one of the many glass houses in Malibu~~ there is a woman who ~~keeps~~ safe the ~~truths~~ about this universe. | Eugene, Oregon kept     lies |

\*Source: Alex Tizon, "My Family's Slave" in *The Atlantic* (June 2017).

# Why This Lost Place

I.

Aurelia adopted a grave
in a nearby cemetery
and makes visits
the 3rd day of each month.
On All Souls Day
she brings pink orange plastic flowers
bought from the corner
98 cents store.
In a small crystal bottle
*kapok* seed oil that's supposed
to keep the shine of the bronze letters
on the memorial marker.

This was not her husband's gravesite.
Here although was a man buried
who had the same first name
and the same year of death
as her husband's
and that was enough.
Two men with the same first names
separated by age
31 years to be exact.
No one asked questions
or was disturbed by her care or attention.
For no one had been visiting °*Francisco Arevalo 1957-1989*°
for years.

She brings along a Polaroid of her husband's gravesite,
lays it right above the raised bronze letters that spell
his first name.
It is a faded pink and white picture
of a tiny marble memorial marker
with a gold cross engraving
on top of the name
°*Francisco Arcacho 1926-1989*°.
Buried in Mandaue in the Arcacho family plot.
He did not know a short visit to
his hometown back in '89
would be an extended one
when he fell sick
and died 4 days
after arriving with his wife.
It was to be a short visit to make up for an absence
spanning 31 years.

Aurelia had to leave him there
and go back to California
promising to send
for his body in a few months.

It has now been at least 5 years
and she has been unable to save
or raise enough money

to have his body brought
back to Los Angeles.
Bearing the cost of a small apartment
poor health and no children to help her
she sends the most of what she can afford,
the $20 equivalent in pesos each month.
It guarantees a small bouquet of roses
put in a glass vase every month.
It guarantees the labor of someone weeding
the grass around the memorial marker.
It also guaranteed the purchase
of a small plastic statue
the *birhen de cebu*
to be placed beside the cross on top of his name.
This money was not sent to family members over there.
It made its way to the cemetery's caretaker each month.
You see, Francisco's long absence from Mandaue did not afford him
the concern or regard from relatives who knew him all but 3 days.
She weeps at this Francisco Arevalo's grave
and wishes
she and her husband had never gone back.
She often weeps at this Francisco Arevalo's grave
and wishes
she never made the promise to bring her husband's body back.

II.

Francisco Arevalo's parents know nothing about a modest grave
in a Los Angeles suburb
where their son's ashes rest.
15 years separate the three from news of baptisms, marriages, lovers,
and illnesses.
A long list updated in diaries both sides will never share.

The mother often comments how the humidity in the Hina coast
has gotten worse
and began the afternoon her son left
many years ago.
The grandmother always had to remind her
*We made him leave.*
*Do not forget that.*
Not once did they ever search for his whereabouts
for they always believed he would come back.

III.

He made Zhang write it down in his diary.
It was the third year of both their illnesses.
*Don't ever send my body back to Hina.*
*Don't ever let anyone from my family know where*
*I'll be laid to rest.*
The promise was kept after he passed on
and for the next three years
Zhang would leave 4 white long-stemmed roses
each month on his lover's grave
and pink orange flowers
on All Saints Day.
Francisco would never know that
when °*Zhang Ling 1957-1992*°
left this world
his body was made to travel eastward
to get buried somewhere else.
Zhang is in the Ling estate mausoleum near Ilang-Ilang.
A Chinese enclave he also made Francisco promise
to never return him to.
But it was Francisco who died first
and that was to be the start of many promises broken.
Zhang's father and mother would not honor the vow they
made to their son.
There was to be no burial beside the man he had spent his life with.

# THE SHAPE OF MY POETRY
## –a gratitude list–

Writing is primarily a solitary activity but context always comes from community. The creative labor spent on this poetry collection spanning 29 years saw the light of day because of a multitudinous number of nurturing and sometimes tough souls who pushed me when pushing was the only way to move me forward and with equal gentleness when that was the only footpath left to get me to my destination. This is where for once, words are powerless to express my deep gratitude to everyone that has been and continues to be part of my creative life.

–my patient ally, tough comrade, best friend ... my love, Evan

–my sweet boys, Max & Papoo and my beautiful girl, Cadi (RIP)

–my parents, my utmost and sincerest gratitude–
Sonia Suico Soriano (RIP) & Clodoveo Valdez Soriano (RIP)

–the Worrall-Soriano family extravaganza I love so dearly–
Anton, Brandy, Moxie, Veo (RIP), Mylo and Chloe

–my birth mother, father and family, til we see each other again–
Erene Romo Murphy, Noeme Murphy Navarro, Jessie Murphy, Steve Murphy, Manuela Romo (RIP) and Andrew Murphy (RIP) ... Francisco R. Suico (RIP) and Vilma Suico Tiu

–my extended family–thank you, thank you for everything–
Sita Sablada (RIP), Manong Miling, Uncle Noel, Auntie Angge and Rinna Soriano, Auntie Josephine Soriano (RIP) and Uncle Donald Ruiz, Uncle Warner Valdez, Auntie Connie Enriquez, Momm Lourdes (RIP), Auntie Merla and Frank Suico, Cesar and Evan Mayol, Cecilia, Melissa, Jayna and Jeff Payo, Ric Parish, Napoleon Lustre and Hector Silva, Karen and Kobey Horn, Miriam, Stuart and Loren Fish, Jon, Rosemary and Steve Saxon, and Peter Brightman

–irreplaceable friendships that sustain–
Karen Kunawicz, Tala Mateo, Celisse Sauceda, Jeannie Shinozuka, Jenny San Angel, Dean & Isela Rizzi, Joel B. Tan, Eric Wat, David Maruyama, Diep Tran, Christina Tam, Wendell Pascual, Allan Aquino, Dorian Merina, Cheryl Deptowicz-Diaz, Jamie Ardeña, Rebecca Baroma, Emily Lawsin, Michelle Magalong, Christine Palma, Marjorie and Shatto Light, Lisa L Somerset, Uncle Henry Peck, Mark Weddington, Lucy Mukerjee-Brown, Natashia Lopez, Martin Wilkey (RIP), Larry Katata, Margarita Alcantara, Elaine Dolalas, Shawn Morrisey, Ming-yuen Ma, Cheryl Seaberg Elliott, Elena Degraaf, J. Allan Warfield, Spiketown crew, Steve Ijams, Cyd Cuniff, Ambi family–Ian Lawrence Tourinho & Erin Gallagher, Bruin Dog crew–Jeri Williams, Paul Park, Shannon Thompson, Tellie Custodio and Jilly Canizares, Nica Aquino & Tina Ford

... MY CIRCLE OF ELATION ...

–I learned how to challenge the world and not accept the status quo, *salamat*–
Professors Holli Levitsky, Sara Chetin, Michael Mageean, Teresa Venegas (RIP), Judith Royer, and Mar Elepano, Mrs. Davis & Mrs. Hadley from Berendo Junior High

–UCLA has been the ideal place for my adult self to flourish. It has been a work environment that has fed me intellectually, sharpened my cultural intuition, and widened my social ties to various communities–so many good people–

>Asian American Studies Center–Don Nakinishi (RIP), Yuji Ichioka (RIP), Emma Gee, Lucy Burns, Keith Camacho, Janet Chen, Sheila Davis, Enrique De La Cruz, Mary Kao, Charles Ku, Marjorie Lee, Betty Leung, Stephanie Santos, Jinqi Ling, Valerie Matsumoto, Tam Nguyen, Arnold Pan, Barbra Ramos, Tritia Toyota, Ming Tu, Melany Dela Cruz-Viesca, Thu-Huong Nguyen-Vo, May Wang, David Yoo, AAPI Dialogues, and all the awesome student workers who have gone through the Center.

>Department of English–Joseph Bristow, Nora Elias, Rick Fagin, Lowell Gallagher, Jeanette Gilkison, Louise Greenberg, Marissa K. Lopez, Danielle Maris, Janel Munguia, Brian Kim Stefans, Wilson Reed, Arvind Thomas, Judith Linde and Pam Weinberger

–I would be remiss if I did not demand an end to animal research in UCLA labs

… MY TRIANGLE OF STRENGTH …

–for continually invigorating my sense of inquiry about the non-human world and being the voices I needed to understand how to share this planet–

>PeeWee (RIP), Ocha (RIP), Max (RIP), Sophie S (RIP), Cadi (RIP), Blackie, Papoose, Sophie B&P (RIP), Lucy B&P (RIP), Fritz, Miller B&P (RIP), and Radar. Clancy (RIP), Cinnamon (RIP), Mr. Sneaky and gang, Joshua (RIP), Scooby (RIP), Ava (RIP), Doodle (RIP), Baxter (RIP) & Peggy Sue, Olive, Dolly (RIP) & Cricket, Leo Bristow, Suzy (RIP), Champ (RIP) & Aloha, Jelly, Shayna, Rex, Moose (RIP), Belly, Chacho, JP, Rudy (RIP), Bella (RIP) & Tenny (RIP), Millie (RIP), Hugger & Kisser (RIP), Tex (RIP), Molson (RIP) & Sandy (RIP), Ginny, Molly (RIP) & Bebe (RIP), Gabriella (RIP), Achilles (RIP), Athena & Ajax, Bucket, Gus-Gus (RIP), Jersey (RIP) & Jelly, Micah and Django, Kuma (RIP), Doodles, Jocko, Sunni (RIP), the rest of the Skov cattery, Cali and all *The Found Dogs* (RIP) that taught the world about tenacity and second chances

–a little stump-tailed macaque named Britches liberated from a University of California, Riverside laboratory in 1985

–for guiding my thinking about veganism, helping build my moral compass, one boycott, one protest, one demo and one rescue at a time–

>Lori Weise, Sandy Dragotis, Robin Skov, Laura Menck, Sharon Tomlin & Mike Manzoori, Alanna Haros & Nick Carranza, Peg Steed, Rin Lennon, Jill Gasparac, Elaine Seamans, Carole Pearson, Dena Delgado, Mindi Memel, Sherri Franklin & Janet Cook. Downtown Dog Rescue Rin's Rescues V.I.P. House, Dimes for Dogs Animals, People and Environment Action aka Ape Action, Precious Pals Pet Rescue, Animal Care for Artists Initiative, Angel's Heart Dog Rescue, Dawg Squad, Southern California Dachshund Relief, Muttville Rescue, At-choo Foundation, No Kill Advocacy Center. Tino Verducci, Rick Bogle, Joshua Harper, Timothy Pachirat, Cory Mac, David Walega, Elvia Sedano, Britt Lind, Nathan J. Winograd and Jim Gorant author of *The Lost Dogs*. Loren Ornelas, Peter Singer, Henry Spira (RIP), Jane Goodall, Steven M. Wise, Lisa Kemmerer, Anuradha Sawhney, Phaik Kee Lim, Rod Coronado, Tom Regan (RIP), Sangduen "Lek" Chailert, Sue Coe and Michael

Budkie. Progress for Science, Art for Animals Sake, Smash HLS, Animal Justice Project, Stop Animal Exploitation Now(SAEN), Food Empowerment Project, People for Reason and Science in Medicine (PRISM), Non-Human Rights Project, Animal Aid Unlimited, Elephant Nature Park, Wolf Patrol, Philippine Animal Welfare Society (PAWS), Backbone Campaign, Amnesty International, Greenpeace, Sea Shepherd Conservation Society & Sahabat Alam Malaysia #seniorrescue #fospicerescue #untileverycageisempty

... MY SPHERE OF COMPASSION ...

*Thou shalt not be a victim, thou shalt not be a perpetrator, but, above all, thou shalt not be a bystander.* —Yehuda Bauer

–for activists who challenge my thinking everyday–
Glenn Omatsu, Manong Philip Veracruz (RIP), Larry Itliong (RIP), Liliosa Hilao (RIP), Uncle Roy Morales (RIP), Silme Domingo (RIP), Gene Viernes (RIP), Gil Mangaoang, Mariame Kaba, Father Luis Olivares (RIP), Keeanga-Yamahtta Taylor, Steve Biko (RIP), Vandana Shiva, Cindy Patton, Hanan al-Shaykh, Alicia Garza, Opal Tometi and Patrisse Cullors, Gary Granada, The Clash, Oscar Romero (RIP), Alex Pacheco, Paul Watson, Kumi Naidoo, Bobby Sands (RIP), Chris Marker (RIP), Emma Goldman (RIP), Bernie Sanders, Amy Goodman, Nana Gyamfi, Rebecca Gomperts, Diana Spencer (RIP), Lav Diaz, Lino Broca (RIP), Ishmael Bernal (RIP), Pete Lacaba, Mike De Leon, Francisco Lombardi, Shinya Tsukamoto, Takeshi Kitano, Lualhati Bautista, Ditsi Carolino and Sari Raissa Lluch Dalena

*Every crisis, actual or impending, needs to be viewed as an opportunity to bring about profound changes in our society. Going beyond protest organizing, visionary organizing begins by creating images and stories of the future that help us imagine and create alternatives to the existing system.* —Grace Lee Boggs

–so many of these writers have inspired me to keep writing and most importantly, finding value in being of service to my community–
Gail Wronsky, F. Sionil Jose, Marisela Norte, Luis Alfaro, Justin Chin, Russell Leong, R. Zamora Linmark, Liz Gonzalez, Nice Rodriguez, Ricky Lee, Eman Lacaba, Jun Lana, Jennifer Tseng, Melissa Roxas, Nana-Ama Danquah, Jolie Chea, Chuck Rosenthal, Roland Tolentino, Zosimo Quibilan Jr., Gretchen Primack, Bryan Thao Worra, Krip Yuson, Nick Carbo and Eileen Tabios, Carlos Bulosan, Richard Adams, Ama Ata Aidoo, Yehudah Amichai, Reinald Arenas, Lorna Dee Cervantes, J.M. Coetzee, Mahmoud Darwish, Carolyn Forche, Anne Frank, Kahlil Gibran, Essex Hemphill Nick Joaquin, Yasunari Kawabata, Wong Kar Wai, Evelyn Lau, Audre Lorde, Janice Mirikitani, Tosha Silver, Charlotte Kasl Sharon Olds, Marge Piercy, Manuel Puig, Susan Sontag, Jose Garcia Villa and Elie Wiesel

–A special thank you to the Festival of Philippine Arts & Culture, Japanese American National Museum, Emerging Voices Program (PEN Center USA), Highways, LadyFest, and *Disorient Journalzine* for supporting my literary pursuits

... ELLIPSES OF LIGHT ...

IRENE SUICO SORIANO was born in Zamboanga del Sur, Philippines, in 1969. At eleven years of age, she and her mother immigrated to Los Angeles, California. Her childhood was spent soaking in the neighborhoods of pre-gentrified Downtown LA, East Hollywood, Rampart/Temple, Melrose, and the Wilshire/Vermont corridor.

She obtained a BA in Creative Writing with an emphasis in Poetry and a minor in Playwriting from Loyola Marymount University. A PEN Center USA Emerging Voices fellow, her poems have appeared in *Philippines Free Press; Solidarity Journal; LA Times; Flippin': Filipinos on America* (Asian American Writers' Workshop); *Babaylan: An Anthology of Filipina and Filipina American Writers* (Aunt Lute); *Short Fuse: The Global Anthology of New Fusion Poetry* (Rattapallax Press); and *Disorient Journalzine,* which published, as part of their Emerging Writers Chapbook Series, her first collection of poetry, *Safehouses.*

She founded and coordinated the Southern California reading series, "Wrestling Tigers: Asian Pacific American Writers Speak" at the Japanese American National Museum and was literary curator for the Los Angeles Festival of Philippine Arts & Culture (FPAC). She was featured in the *Los Angeles Times* for her curatorial participation in the ground-breaking NEA-funded World Beyond Poetry Festival that featured over 100 poets from the diverse communities of LA, and co-produced, as part of the LA Enkanto Art Collective, the CD *In Our Blood: Filipina/o American Poetry & Spoken Word from Los Angeles.*

She is the founder of Bark & Purr Alliance Fund, which makes available resources to aid the rescue of geriatric and terminally ill dogs and cats that enter LA's city and county shelter system. She participates in local and international anti-vivisection efforts and believes in the fundamental rights of non-human animals to live and be free from harm, pain, exploitation, and captivity.

Irene lives in the San Fernando Valley with her two rescued dogs, Papoo and Maxon, and her significant human, Evan.

Instagram + Twitter: @archipelagopoem

# NOTES

# NOTES

# NOTES

# NOTES

# NOTES

# NOTES

# NOTES

# NOTES

# NOTES

# NOTES

# NOTES

www.ingramcontent.com/pod-product-compliance
Lightning Source LLC
LaVergne TN
LVHW051508070426
835507LV00022B/2984